Succeed Your Startup 2.0

Succeed Your Startup 2.0

Issame Hamaoui

© 2015 - Issame HAMAOUI

Edition: BoD - Books on Demand
12/14 rond-point des Champs Elysées
75008 Paris

Printed by **BoD** – **B**ooks **o**n **D**emand, Norderstedt
ISBN: **978-2-3220-1445-3**
Cover page designed by **Freepik.com**

Contents

1. **The idea** _____ 7
   - 1.1 Find a good idea _____ 7
   - 1.2 Validate your idea _____ 9
   - 1.3 Protect your idea _____ 13
   - 1.4 Business Plan _____ 17

2. **Formulate the idea** _____ 19
   - 2.1 Specifications _____ 19
   - 2.2 Mockups _____ 20
   - 2.3 The graphic charter _____ 21
   - 2.4 Surround yourself with the right people _____ 21

3. **Creating a website** _____ 22
   - 3.1 Hand coding _____ 22
   - 3.2 CMS (Content Management System) _____ 23
   - 3.3 Website builders _____ 24
   - 3.4 Agency & IT services company & Freelancer _____ 25
   - 3.5 Conclusion _____ 26

4. **Designing a mobile application** _____ 27
   - 4.1 Native approach _____ 27
   - 4.2 Web-based approach _____ 31
   - 4.3 Hybrid approach _____ 33

5. **Various legal formalities** _____ 37
   - 5.1 Legal notices _____ 37
   - 5.2 Declaration to a data protection authorities _____ 38
   - 5.3 Personal information gathering _____ 39
   - 5.4 Business structure _____ 40

6. **The publication of website/application** _____ 43
   - 6.1 Website hosting _____ 43
   - 6.2 Publication of the mobile application: _____ 45

7. **Increase website/application traffic** _____ 46
   - 7.1 Introduction _____ 46
   - 7.2 Natural SEO (Search Engine Optimization) _____ 46

- 7.3 Pay Per Click (PPC) _____ 48
- 7.4 Get social _____ 50
- 7.5 E-mailing _____ 51
- 7.6 The Video Marketing _____ 52
- 7.7 Create a blog for website/mobile application _____ 53
- 7.8 Promote dialogue _____ 53
- 7.9 Viral Marketing _____ 54
- 7.10 Conclusion_____ 54

8. **Web analytics** _____ 55
- 8.1 Definition _____ 55
- 8.2 Web Analytics: Metrics & Key Performance Indicators 55
- 8.3 Web Analytics tools _____ 57

9. **Funding** _____ 64
- 9.1 Fund your startup yourself _____ 64
- 9.2 Pitch your needs to friends and family _____ 64
- 9.3 Request a small-business grant _____ 65
- 9.4 Seek a bank loan or credit-card line of credit ____ 65
- 9.5 Start a crowdfunding campaign online _____ 65
- 9.6 Solicit investors _____ 65
- 9.7 Join a startup incubator or accelerator _____ 65
- 9.8 Enter a competition _____ 66

10. **Business models (monetization)** _____ 67
- 10.1 Paid app _____ 67
- 10.2 Pay Per Click Advertising Networks_____ 68
- 10.3 Affiliate Marketing _____ 68
- 10.4 Set up an online store _____ 69
- 10.5 Services/Consulting/Coaching_____ 69
- 10.6 Data Monetization _____ 69
- 10.7 Freemium _____ 70
- 10.8 Sell your application to someone else _____ 70
- 10.9 Donation / Becoming a sponsor _____ 70

1. The idea

1.1 Find a good idea

You want to create your startup, but you have not yet found the idea? Here are some tips to follow to get a good idea that will make the difference.

1.1.1 Cultivate a passion

Our passions and our interests are a great source of startup's ideas, because they are obviously things we like to do with enthusiasm and without getting bored.

Note explicitly in a notepad all of your interests without restriction: I like cooking; I like sports news; etc.... The goal here is to have a maximum of keywords that interest you; they will be used to find the right idea.

1.1.2 Identify an unmet need and fill it

We must improve our ability to observe, our criticism and our openness of mind.

- By observing our environment, we can identify exiting problems and the reasons why they exist.
- A critical mind allows us to question what already exists, in order to consider possible approaches of enhancement to improve our lives and those of others.
- Finally, the openness of mind will help us acquiring a wider comprehension of the environment around us so we can develop more inspiration.

1.1.3 Import an existing concept from abroad

Nowadays, it is difficult to invent a new concept. How to innovate when almost everything already exist? A solution is offered to us by adapting a concept that does not exist in our country, but succeeded in other countries.

We can look for ideas abroad in order to adapt them to our market, without neglecting the barriers like the difference of cultures or the maturity of markets. Some concepts are imported very well especially in the Internet field.

Example:
- PriceMinister.com was born based on the American Half.com, then bought by the Japanese Rakuten for 270 millions of dollars.

1.1.4 Transpose a concept to another sector

After observation and identification of an innovative concept that has been proven, we can imagine its use in another industry.

So, we should identify successful ideas and reuse them according to our interests and opportunities.

Examples:
- Groupon for urban women ➔ Dealissime
- Facebook for pets ➔ Yummypets
- Firefox for children ➔ Potati
- Linkedin for young graduates ➔ Yupeek

1.1.5 Conclusion

To help you finding a good idea to start a business, the non-exhaustive list below may be helpful:

- Websites of innovative new business ideas and trends: springwise.com, techcrunch.com, whogotfunded.com, coolbusinessideas.com, etc.
- Websites of popular innovative start-up incubators: 500.co/startups, ilab.harvard.edu, http://www.inc.com/ss/10-start-up-incubators-to-watch, etc.
- Business magazines: thestartupmag, Entrepreneur, sbomag, arabianbusiness, frenchweb, etc. provide regularly many new business ideas.
- Start-up competitions: leweb.co, startupopen.com, etc.

1.2 Validate your idea

Before embarking and commit time and money to create our startup, it is very important to check the validity of our idea. This is a primary step that will allow us to avoid disappointment.

I propose a stepwise approach to validate your idea.

1.2.1 Determine the components of the idea

An idea is not enough to develop a project. The main idea must be accompanied by a reflection on the following questions:

- What services / concepts, do we want to produce or exploit?
- What need does the concept meet or problem does it help solve?
- What will be the way in which the concept / service is used?
- How it will be sold?
- What is the innovative feature of the service / concept (if there is one)?
- What are its strengths?
- What are its weaknesses?

1.2.2 Define the target market

This step provides a broad idea about the target audience. For this, we must answer the following questions:

- **What is the nature of the market targeted?** Local, regional, national or international? Permanent or seasonal? Etc.
- **Which customer do you expect you can reach?** Young employees? Retired? Craft businesses? Small and medium enterprises? Large groups? Liberal cabinets? Property managers? Various agencies, etc.
- **What is the identified target?** At this stage, we should be able to describe what could be our major client base.

1.2.3 Describe the activity very accurately

Now - thanks to the questions posed above – we must be able to write accurately in a few sentences the activity of our startups.

This exercise will save a lot of time to write our business plan later.

1.2.4 Seek advice and guidance

It is very important to talk about our project to professionals; they can advise us and give us an informed and neutral look. So, do not hesitate to approach with caution:

- Chambers of commerce in your country,
- Young entrepreneurs associations,
- Clubs,
- Incubators,
- Accelerators,
- Business angels,
- Family,
- Friends,
- Etc.

1.2.5 Analyse the constraints

We should identify all the constraints and risks, with the purpose to eliminate or reduce them. Below, we'll identify the most known:

a. Constraints on the nature of the concept/service
- Complex: development time, standards to meet.
- Innovative: requires changing the habits of users.
- Easy to duplicate: risk of introduction of large competitors, requires to occupy as quickly as possible the market.
- Very expensive: hesitation among potential buyers.
- Not profitable in itself: income generated by third parties.

- Dependant: on key partners.
- Latest fad: what's next?
- Negative image: requires strong communication strategy.

b. Market constraints
- The market is to create? Is starting up? Very fast growing? Mature? In decline? ...
- Are there barriers to entry?
- The market is fragmented, too wide, very risky, inconstant, slow and unresponsive, long time to payment, etc....?
- Is there a risk of emergence of powerful competitors with a lot of resources, or to be encountered by anti-competitive practices?

c. Regulatory constraints
- Do we have the experience or qualifications required?
- Can we get the required approvals (copyright, royalty-free images...) and did we verify that the activity is not under regulation?
- If we are employees, did our employment contract contain restrictions to perform the activity?

d. Resources constraints
- We should identify the technical, human and financial resources to achieve our projects.

1.2.6 Define the personal project of the entrepreneur

To put all the chances on our side, it is very important to check if there is coherence between the requirements of our project and:

- **Our personality**: rigorous, serious, sociable, shy, extrovert, introvert, strict, charismatic...
- **Our potential**: good physical and mental condition, capacity to absorb stress, negotiation skills, resourceful, creative and responsive, ability to develop relational networks, to communicate, to lead...

- **Our motivations**: desire for independence, a taste of the responsibilities and challenges, concretize a dream or a passion, fully realize potentials and change lives, exploit interesting opportunities, improve condition and quality of life, earn income immediately, increase revenues…
- **Our goals**: work alone, build a company of dozens of employees in few years, earn great revenue, resell quickly the startup, become leader…
- **Our skills and knowledge**: ideally technical, commercial and management.
- **Our personal constraints**: availability and time, financial constraints, borrowing capacity, health…

1.2.7 Verify the realism of the idea

Using previously gathered information; we can measure the realism and feasibility of the idea through the SWOT matrix, which allows analysing the strengths, weaknesses, opportunities and threats of our project:

- **Strengths**: the concept meets a real need, sufficient and accessible market, existing clients to start, innovative nature, unified and experienced team …
- **Weaknesses**: financial resources, low motivation, little time, risk of being dependent, cultural resistance from customers, no experience, no references / partners …
- **Threats**: legal and regulatory risks, lack of reputation compared to competitors …
- **Opportunities**: advertising revenue, customer loyalty easier…

Following this line of thought, we should be able to conclude whether the project is realistic, in which case we must embark, or otherwise abandon.

1.3 Protect your idea

Protecting an idea is not required as such, but when wanting to present the project to investors or partners without fear, the protection become essential.

An idea cannot be protected; only its expression can, through different types of intellectual properties protection available.

1.3.1 Choosing a name

A relevant name is the best guarantee of our successful startup, it is essential to choose it the simplest way possible.

Below are given some criteria to choose an appropriate name:

- Available: the name must not be the property of a third party:
    - http://www.kompass.com/selectcountry/: To check out the availability of a company name in the same activity sector.
    - http://knowem.com/checktrademarkavailability.php: To check the availability of the brand name.
    - http://domai.nr/: To check the availability of the domain name in major international extensions (.com, .net, .eu...)
    - http://www.namechk.com: To check whether the name has already been registered in social networks.
- Short, simple, easy to remember and write in all target languages.
- Successfully represent our business without being too restrictive.

https://adwords.google.com/KeywordPlanner: Google Adwords Keyword Planner – a free tool that helps us to find keywords by relevance and popularity, and to estimate their competitiveness and volume of searches.

1.3.2 Registering a domain name

ICANN (Internet Corporation for Assigned Names and Numbers) is the authority that manages domain names extensions (.com, .net, .org…). This organisation delegates the registration and management of domain names to "Registries": for example, .com management is ensured by the American company VERISIGN, .eu by the non-profit organisation EURID. These registries, in turn, are based on accredited companies called "Registrars", that provide direct sale to the final customer.

The main registrars are gandi.net, name.com, ovh.com and 1and1 (http://www.internic.net/regist.html).

Any domain name is created for at least 1 year and not more than 10 years. However, it is possible at any time to extend the lifetime of a domain name.

1.3.3 Protecting software/application/website

Ideas and concepts cannot be protected as such. Only the achievement of this idea or that concept can be protected:

1.3.3.1 Apply for a patent

A patent is a legal title of industrial property granting its owner the exclusive right to exploit an invention commercially for a limited area and time. It confers its owner the right to prevent others from commercially using such invention (e.g., production, application, selling, importing) without authorization.

Cost: The maintenance of a patent over 20 years costs an average of: 20,000$ in United States of America and 32,000€ in Europe.

Term of protection: 20 years

1.3.3.2 Registering a trademark

A trademark is a sign (word, logo, symbol, slogan, colour, shape, etc....) capable of distinguishing the products or services of a person or of a group of persons. Acquire an exclusive right on trademark allows to prevent any natural or legal person to use this distinctive sign in the protected sectors (classes).

Term of protection: 10 years indefinitely renewable.

Contact: http://www.uspto.gov/ (united states)

1.3.3.3 Deposit of designs

Software/application/website ergonomics may be protected by a deposit of designs.

Term of protection: 10 years.

Contact: http://www.uspto.gov/ (united states)

1.3.3.4 Copyright

Software, web sites, applications, etc. are protected under the convention of literary and artistic property. Copyright protection is automatic as soon as there is a record in any form of what has been created (there is no official registration). However, steps can be taken by the creator of a work to provide evidence that he or she had the work at a particular time:

- The creator could send himself or herself a copy by **special delivery post** (which gives a clear date stamp on the envelope), leaving the envelope unopened on its return.
- A copy could be deposited with a **bank or solicitor**.
- A number of **private companies** operate unofficial registers, but it would be sensible to check carefully what you will be paying for before choosing this route.

It is important to note, that this does not prove that a work is original or created by you. But it may be useful to be able to show that the work was in your possession at a particular date, for example where someone else claims that you have copied something of theirs that was only created at a later date.

1.4 Business Plan

The Business Plan is a reflection tool that allows formalizing, organizing and planning the project. It is also a communication tool to present precisely and clearly our startup to various stakeholders (partners, bankers, investors, franchisors, aids, competitions...).

Below the main topics that should be covered by a Business Plan:

- **The portrait of the startup:** Define all facets and related subjects to the startup – legal form, location, starting date of the activity, capital, etc....
- **The team:** Present the project leader and all key people in the startup (summarized resumes). The purpose is to show the complementarity, experience and cohesion of the team, as well as it meets all the necessary skills.
- **The products and/or services:** What needs does it meet? What is the existing offer? What is the innovative nature of products/services, advantages and disadvantages compared to the existing offer? Why they were not already offered? Is the market mature?
- **The market:**
    o Demonstrate the existence of a market (prospects and customers surveys)
    o Identify potential clients.
    o Define clearly the geographical areas targeted.
    o Examine the prospects for development of the market.
- **The business model:**
    o Define the major sources of income for the startup.
    o Specify the distribution channels.
    o Define the selling price of the products/services.
    o Define the business strategy.
- **Funding:**
    o Financing plan: financial needs and expected sources of funding (capital, grants, loans...).
    o Forecast results, cash-flow statement and liquidity plans (for the first year, 3 years, and 5 years).

- **The competition:**
    - List all direct or indirect competitors.
    - Indicate for each competitor: age, size, turnover, market share, characteristics of the product/service, reputation, etc.
    - Enhance competitive advantages.
    - Define the entry barriers for new entrants.
- **Marketing and sales strategy:**
    - Set prices for products and/or services.
    - Establish a marketing and communication strategy (media, budget, campaigns, partnerships, etc.)
    - Establish a commercial strategy (distribution channels, delivery dates and payment terms, sales policy, etc.)

There are several simple and practical templates that help to write a business plan, you can find some good examples on the magazine's website entrepreneur.com
http://www.entrepreneur.com/formnet/businessplantemplates.html

2. Formulate the idea

2.1 Specifications

When we want to create a startup around a web or mobile concept, it is very important to write clear and detailed specifications. This will hopefully give good guidance in technical developments.

A specification is a document allowing to exhaustively define the basic features of the application/website. It contains the list of needs, requirements and constraints that must be met during the project. It must also contain all the elements to measure the cost, time, human resources and quality assurance.

Specifications must include three main categories:
- **Presentation of needs**: we should give a brief project description - explain exactly what it is about, the problem, the purpose, the planning, the scope, etc.
- **Functional analysis**: we should make a complete study of the different features of the application/website:
    - Identify and list all the expected functionalities and their constraints.
    - Describe the functions sequences.
    - Represent the extended features models.
    - ⇨ Some tools to achieve this analysis: « APTE - The Horned Beast », « APTE - The Octopus » …
- **The proposed solution to meet the needs:** we should suggest solutions to accomplish each feature. The objective is to better organize the project by dividing it into several parts 'sub projects' and listing the different ideas that can help to meet the needs.

P.S.: Keep it simple and offer only the features that perfectly meet the needs of your customers (Google, YouTube, Twitter, etc. are simple tools)

2.2 Mockups

After defining the need that must be met by the project and the main expected features, we can design the website/application **mockup**.

A graphical mockup, also known as a prototype or wireframe is a visual guide that depicts the page layout or arrangement of the website's/application's content, including interface elements and navigational systems, and how they work together. It focuses on what a screen does, not what it looks like.

There are many wireframing tools, which combine ease of handling and speed of implementation. The following are some of the more common and frequently used:
- http://balsamiq.com/
- http://mockupbuilder.com/
- https://wireframe.cc/
- https://gomockingbird.com/mockingbird/#
- http://www.mockflow.com/

These tools make possible to create accurately interactive mockups (by defining the sequence of actions and interactions with clickable links on different objects: buttons, links, images, etc.)

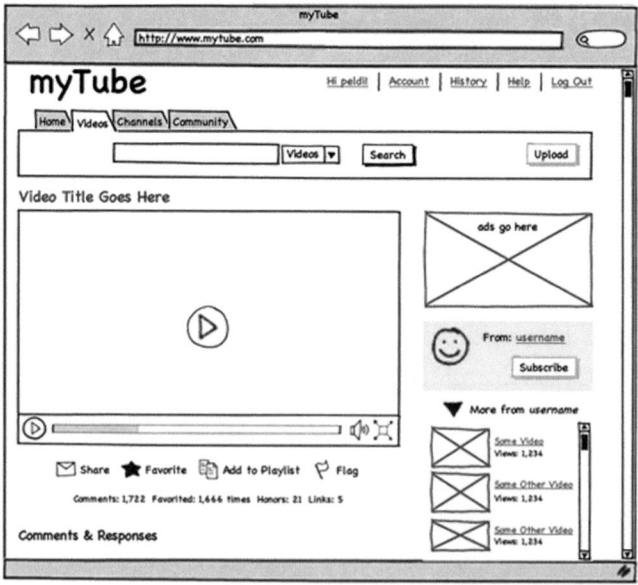

2.3 The graphic charter

The graphic charter is a document containing the rules regarding the graphic identity of a project, company or organisation. It defines the overall graphic, iconographic, typographic and ergonomic guidelines that should be followed on the website/application. It can be used by various communications channels (newsletters, sales brochure, flyers, business cards, etc.…)

Creating a graphic charter includes:
- Creating logo (colours, forms, shapes),
- Creating banner,
- Selecting fonts to use,
- Selecting colours (primary, secondary, text, links...),
- Creating illustrations and images,
- Etc.…

2.4 Surround yourself with the right people

As startup, we're still trying to understand how our business models will work, who our real customers are, and how our products (or services) best function. It's hard to find those answers when we surround ourselves with other people with similar profiles.

So, when the startup is co founded, we must emphasize complementarity – a cohesive team unified by shared goals can stand up to all encountered challenges.

That is why we need to find business partners that can bridge the gap in knowledge. We can use dedicated professional networks and communities of entrepreneurs like: Viadeo.com, linkedin.com, biznik.com, cmypitch.com, cofoundr.com, econnect.entrepreneur.com, partnerUp.com, startupNation.com, xing.com …

3. Creating a website

Once the specifications, mockups and graphical charts are ready, we can start building the website: we know exactly the deliverables to be produced and we have already defined the precise planning. This will allow us to increase productivity and quality.

Many solutions are available to help us create our website:

3.1 Hand coding

Manually creating and designing a website is a process that involves the implementation of necessary means and important skills. A website can be a simple HTML page, or thousands of pages offering animations, services developed using PHP (or another server-side programming language), JavaScript and AJAX forms. It can also include the use of a database, for example MySQL.

Below you will find some of essential tools that help to effectively and qualitatively develop a website:
- **Notepad++**: is one of the most popular text/code editors for Windows users. It is a full-featured, free, open source, really fast and reliable. It supports syntax highlighting and code folding for over 50 programing, scripting, and markup languages. It has a huge range of simple and pertinent features, very helpful when writing code.
- **MySQL Workbench:** is a visual database design tool that integrates SQL development, administration, database design, creation and maintenance into a single integrated development environment for the MySQL database system.
- **Photoshop:** is the most well-known and widely used graphics editing software. There are plenty of completely free alternatives to Photoshop, here are a few of the best: Gimp2, Adob Photoshop Express, PixLr, Paint.NET, PicMonkey, etc...

- **FileZilla:** is free, fast and reliable FTP client with lots of useful features and an intuitive interface. It is useful for transferring files from our home computer to our website server.

3.2 CMS (Content Management System)

A CMS (**C**ontent **M**anagement **S**ystem) is a computer application that allows publishing, editing and modifying content, organizing, deleting as well as maintenance from a central interface.

CMS's are usually free and written in PHP, it is installed on the server side and a SQL database is needed to make it work.

Advantages:
- **Open source & Free:** CMS's are in most cases free and open source.
- **Easy to use:** CMS allows to create a website without knowing a programming language.
- **Fast handling:** CMS's are intuitive and quick to manage.
- **A community:** Most popular CMS' have a large community of users and developers. It makes it easy to find the answers we need.
- **Modular:** Most CMS's are modular, they consist of a design that uses components and modules that we can add or delete according to our needs.
- **Customizable themes:** Thanks to themes and templates, CMS's allow to easily and quickly customize our website design.

Disadvantages:
- **Lack of basic features**: CMS does not always meet all of our needs. In some cases, we will even have to hand code to create the desired functionality.
- **Security**: The source code is available for everybody, so flaws.
- **Performance:** a CMS designed website is often less efficient and therefore slower than a hand coding one (connection to the database, retrieving content, etc....)

Examples:
- **Blog**: Wordpress, DotClear
- **Wiki**: MediaWiki, PmWiki
- **Website**: Joomla, Spip, Drupal
- **Social network**: Jomsocial, SocialEngine, BuddyPress
- **Ecommerce website**: Prestashop, Drupal e-commerce, WP e-commerce, VirtueMart, Magento
- **Forum**: PhpBB, fluxBB

3.3 Website builders

Website builders are tools that allow the construction of websites without manual code editing. They are online proprietary tools provided by web hosting companies, typically intended for users to build their private site.

Advantages:
We can quickly create our website without any technical skills (languages PHP, HTML, CSS, etc....). Also, we can start an online business without putting out a penny (no domain name or hosting to pay for)

Disadvantages:
The number of pages, the website hosting size and the design selections are limited. Similarly, a website created using a builder will not have its own domain name, but rather as "myWebSite.blogger.com" or "sites.google.com/myWebSite".

Examples:
- Blog: blogger.com, wordpress.com
- Website: sites.google.com, www.weebly.com
- Social network: ning.com, grou.ps
- Ecommerce website: weezbe.com, prestabox.com, shopify.com

3.4 Agency & IT services company & Freelancer

While creating our website, we may have recourse to an external party. We have the choice between: a freelancer, a web design agency or an IT services company.

3.4.1 Freelancer

A freelancer or freelance worker is a self-employed person working in a profession or trade in which full-time employment is also common. Freelancers work in a variety of professions, they can be web designers, integrators, developers or all that at the same time. For small projects such as showcase website, he can do the work alone and for an interesting cost.

The biggest platforms for finding freelancers are: odesk.com, freelancer.com, elance.com.

3.4.2 Web design agency

A web agency is a company specialized in the design and implementation of websites. It consists essentially of specialists such as project managers, web designers, integrators, web developers, SEO, community managers and marketers. Consequently, web agencies are praised for their professionalism and their ability to handle large projects easily.

3.4.3 IT services company

The IT services outsourcing company is not generally specialized in web design, otherwise it would be called web design agency.

If we already rely on one of these companies, then it will be interesting to subcontract the building of our website to it. So we continue to work with our normal point of contact, he knows us and we know him, that is reassuring. A disadvantage is that generally the prices of IT services companies are higher than those of agencies and freelancers.

3.5 Conclusion

The question to ask is "what are my needs?". In most cases, a CMS perfectly satisfies our needs, and it is unnecessary to develop a solution for months. However, if we want a website with very specific features, and we have available sufficient technical expertise, budget and time, then we can choose
a custom solution (hand-coding, freelance, web design agency, etc.)

4. Designing a mobile application

The implementation of a mobile application should take into account a number of important elements, such as the diversity of operating systems (iOS, Android, Windows Phone...), the multitude of different hardware (Apple, Samsung, HTC, Nexus...), the ergonomics, native application vs. web application, etc.

In this section, we will try to provide some useful food for thought about the development of mobile applications. So, we afford a clear overview on this subject to better understand the strengths and limitations of existing solutions and to be able to make good choices.

When developing for mobile platforms, there are three possible approaches: native, web and hybrid.

4.1 Native approach

4.1.1 Introduction

The native approach consists of using solely the platform's software development toolkit to build an application that is compiled to the platform's native language. Currently, the most prominent platforms are Android, iOS and Windows Phone.

This approach enable the developer to build native applications, with access to all the capabilities of the smartphone, such as camera, GPS, sensors, hardware acceleration, etc. and an excellent user experience.

4.1.2 iOS (iPhone OS)

Thanks to the success of Apple, developing applications for the iOS platform - which means targeting the iPhone, iPod and iPad devices - has become increasingly popular.

Hardware and programming language:
- **Mac:** Developing applications for iPhone requires a Mac (or Mac Mini)
- **Xcode:** is an integrated development environment (IDE) containing a suite of software development tools developed by Apple for developing software for OS X and iOS. We can register for free as an apple developer https://developer.apple.com/register/index.action to
download XCode. If desired, we can register to the paid program of Apple "iOS Developer Program" which enables us signing our application, running it on our device and publish it on App Store. But to just try developing on iOS, a free account is quite sufficient.
- **Objective-C:** is the language used to code native applications for Mac OS X and iPhone.

Learn more: http://www.appcoda.com/ios-programming-course/

Publishing on the App Store: Once developed, the application must be submitted for approval by Apple. It is then added to the App Store, upon payment of a license to install it on iPhone (99$ per year for individuals, 300$ per year for companies)

4.1.3 Android

The world of mobile application development was upset by the launch of the open-source mobile operating system Android, which has quickly become the most popular in the world.

Hardware and programming language:
- **Hardware:** In general, any computer enables developing on Android, so we can use Windows, Mac OS X or any Linux distribution.
- **JDK:** (Java **D**evelopment **K**it) is a software development environment used for developing Java applications. It includes the Java Runtime Environment (JRE), an interpreter/loader (java), a compiler (javac), an archive (jar), a documentation generator (javadoc) and other tools needed in Java development.

- **Android SDK**: (Android Software Development Kit) includes a comprehensive set of development tools. These include a debugger, libraries, emulators, documentation, sample code, and tutorials.
- **Android Studio**: is an integrated development environment (IDE) dedicated entirely to Android. Previously, Eclipse has been Google's recommended IDE for Android, but now the search giant is shaking things up by giving developers a choice of supported development environments. Both IDEs are free and available for Windows, Mac OS X and Linux.
- **Java**: is the programming language used to develop native applications for Android.

Learn more: http://developer.android.com/training/index.html

Publishing on Google Play: To publish our applications on Google Play, we must register for a Google Play publisher account and pay a $25 USD registration fee (one time only).

4.1.4 Windows Phone

With a slight delay behind iPhone and Android, Microsoft attacks the mobility market with a little more maturity and proposes its mobile operating system: Windows Phone.

Hardware and programming language:
- **Hardware**: We should have Windows 7, Windows Vista SP2 or Windows 8 which are for the moment the only supported configurations allowing to develop for Windows Phone.
- **Visual Studio 2010 Express**: is a set of freeware integrated development environments (IDE) provided by Microsoft as a lightweight and free version of the paid Visual Studio. The idea of Express editions is to provide streamlined, easy-to-use and easy-to-learn IDEs for hobbyists and students to start developing for Windows Phone.

- **Windows Phone SDK**: are software development kits from Microsoft that contain tools required to develop applications or games for Windows Phone.
- **C#**: is the flagship programming language designed by Microsoft and allows the creation of computer applications of all kinds.

Learn more: http://channel9.msdn.com/Series/Windows-Phone-7-Development-for-Absolute-Beginners

Publication on Windows Phone Store: That's it, our application is ready. To publish it on Windows Phone Store, we must register for a developer account, which costs 99$ per year.

4.2 Web-based approach

4.2.1 Introduction

The web-based mobile app approach, modern web technologies like HTML5, CSS3 and JavaScript frameworks are used. This gives us the possibility to create cross-platform applications accessible via web browser.

In contrast, the mobile web does not allow access to high performances or to lower layers of the device and many functions of the hardware can be accessed only partially, slowly or not at all. Ergonomics is not perfectly suited to smartphone, and the access to our application is done only via the web browsers.

4.2.2 Hand coding

A web mobile application is simply a website suitable for mobile devices. It doesn't need to be downloaded from stores and installed on smartphones or tablets, as it is a simple website accessible via web browsers like Chrome, Safari, Firefox, Opera...

Here are some basic principles that we must follow when creating a mobile version of our main website:
- **Optimizing page layout**: It is important to reduce the content displayed in mobile website's pages and ensure that the information is easy to access.
- **Pages and navigation:** The clear and intuitive navigation becomes essential, because users always seek to perform tasks quickly and efficiently.
- **Pages size:** The maximum size of a page from a mobile version of the site should not exceed 20KB. The purpose is to increase the speed of loading pages and reduce costs for visitors with paying connections.
- **Domain name:** there is no need to host the mobile version separately on another domain. Most mobile websites are hosted on subdomains. (http://mobi.mywebsite.com)

- **Compatibility:** we should avoid Flash, Silverlight, Java applet, audio, video, pop-ups, JavaScript ... because they are not (or scarcely) compatible with mobile browsers.

There are several Frameworks based on HTML5/JavaScript/CSS technologies that enable to create web applications compatible with most recent mobile devices (iPhone, Android, Windows Phone, BlackBerry, etc.) and suitable for all screen resolutions.

The main interest of these frameworks is to allow developers to code quickly and easily mobile web applications thanks to available components (forms, lists, tables...)

The most successful (in my opinion) Frameworks are:
- JQuery Mobile: http://jquerymobile.com/
- Sencha Touch: http://www.sencha.com/products/touch
- M-Project: http://www.the-m-project.org/
- JQTouch: http://jqtjs.com/
- Wink: http://www.winktoolkit.org/
- DaVinci Studio: http://www.davincisdk.com/?page_id=9

4.2.3 CMS: Mobile plugin

If our website is built around a CMS, it is then possible to find a free extension, which provides a mobile version suitable for smartphones (Android, iPhone, Windows Phone, BlackBerry, etc....)

The principle is simple. The plugin detects the browser's type of our website's visitor, and if it is a smartphone, then the mobile version of the website will be displayed (screen size, loading speed, template, etc....)

Examples:
- Wordpress: « WP Touch » plugin.
- Joomla: « Mobile Joomla » extension.
- Drupal: « Mobile Plugin » module.
- Magento: « Magento Connect » extension.

4.3 Hybrid approach

4.3.1 Introduction

It is the combination of the "native" approach and the "web-based" approach. The hybrid approach allows the development of native mobile apps (Android, iOS, Windows Phone, BlackBerry OS, etc....) by using pure web languages: HTML5, CSS and JavaScript.

Many hybrids frameworks dedicated to mobility have been developed, the most successful are: PhoneGap and Appcelerator. They offer a bridge between JavaScript and the lower layers, which provides access to more features on smartphones.

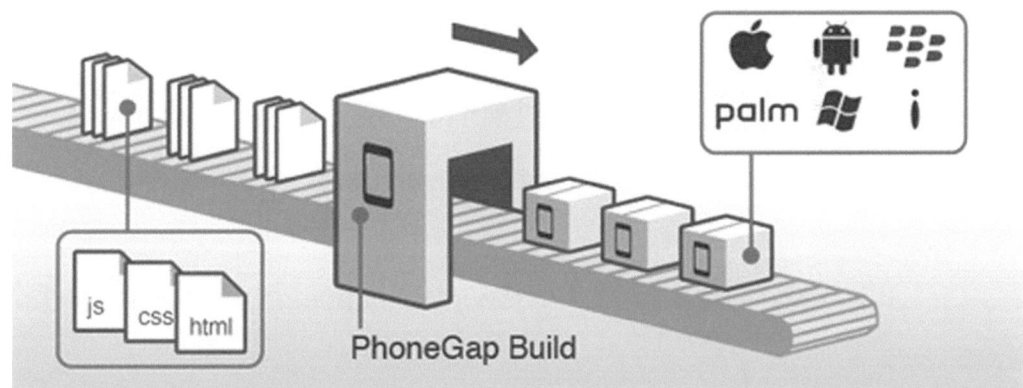

4.3.2 PhoneGap

The PhoneGap framework, also known as Apache Cordova is an open-source JavaScript API able to interact with the API of mobile devices (location, vibration, accelerometer, sound files, contact list, etc....)

Learn more: http://phonegap.com/

Configuration

PhoneGap requires installation and configuration of several environments according on platforms on which we want to develop our application. For example, to create an iPhone application we will need a Mac, the Xcode software and PhoneGap iOS SDK.

Advantages:
- Free.
- Open source with large support (IMB, Apache, Adobe, RIM, etc.….).
- Re-usability and portability of code with minimal change (Code once, deploy everywhere).
- Supportive for all major platforms.
- Support for various API's (Accelerometer, Geo location, media, network, camera, storage, etc.).
- Large community (plugins, tutorials).
- Web skills Reusable.
- Saving time and reducing development costs.

Disadvantages:
- It is "only" a JavaScript API: the implementation of callback methods is a substantial workload.
- Debugging becomes difficult.
- Several development environments are required.
- The applications are web applications inside a Web-View. Browser performance doesn't come close to native application component performance.
- Because it's covering multiple platforms, PhoneGap is often one step behind the native platforms when new features are introduced.
- The look and feel of the mobile app created by using PhoneGap might not be the same as the platform specific mobile app.

Adobe provides an online tool called "PhoneGap Build" to allow developers to easily compile, build and package their apps to all target platforms by simply upload HTML5, CSS and JavaScript assets (without installing any software). https://build.phonegap.com/

4.3.3 Appceleretor Titanium

Titanium is an open-source framework that allows the creation of mobile apps on platforms including iOS, Android, Windows Phone, BlackBerry OS, and Tizen from a single JavaScript codebase.

Learn more: http://www.appcelerator.com/developers/

Configuration:
Titanium provides a dedicated IDE, based on Aptana, one of the best Web IDE based itself on Eclipse.

Advantages:
- Free.
- Open source.
- Tons of features.
- Supports multiple platforms in single code base.
- Allows developing native mobile apps using our web skills.
- Only one development environment for all platforms.
- Better performance than PhonGap.
- Can be extended to add in any native feature.

Disadvantages:
- Few platforms supported.
- Good JavaScript skills are required.
- Developers need to learn the Titanium API.
- The Titanium IDE requires a permanent Internet connection.
- Poor documentation and lack of learning resources.
- Debugging becomes difficult.

4.3.4 Conclusion

Here is a very effective decision tree that will help us choosing the best approach for our mobile application:

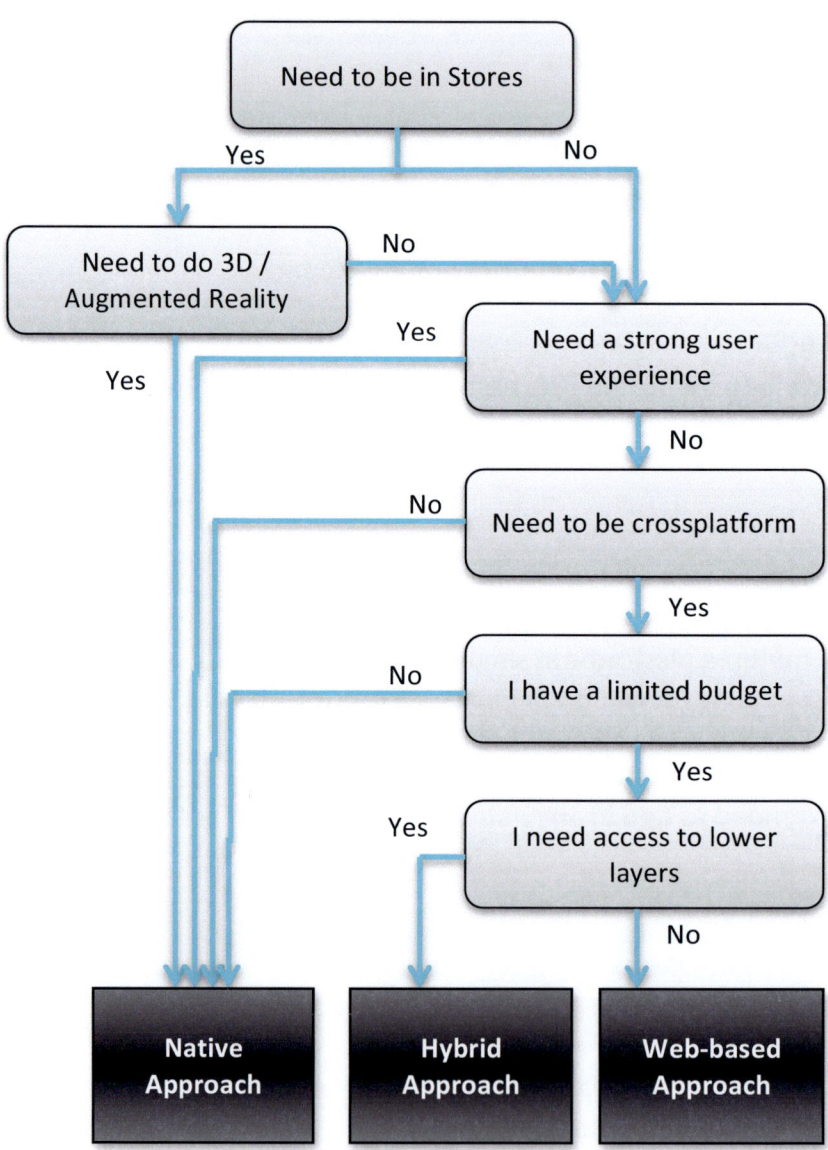

5. Various legal formalities

The web site and/or the mobile application is now developed. It is therefore necessary to consider the legal aspects before launching our business.

5.1 Legal notices

All websites and mobile applications should include a section entitled: **Legal notices**. This is the first of formalities.
This section should summarize the following information:

Individual: an individual with a blog, a website or a personal mobile application must also be submitted to the publication of legal obligations:
- First name
- Last name
- Home address
- Phone number
- If available: the company registration number (This number is used to identify our company alone).

However, it is possible to retain anonymity, only if the exact contact information on the person in charge of the website/ application has been transmitted to the host.

It is imperative to add to the Legal notices page - regardless of status (individual or company) - information relating to the hosting of the website:
- Web hosting name,
- Company name,
- Address,
- Phone number

Company: a professional webSite / application must include multiple mandatory information:
- Business name or company name,
- Headquarters,

- Phone number,
- The name of The managing editor of the Website,
And if available:
- Legal structure,
- Social capital (if legal structure),
- VAT number and the company registration number.

Online stores: in addition to legal notices, they must add other mandatory information:
- The General Terms and Conditions of Sale
- The delivery conditions
- The payment terms

There are simple and free online tools that allow us to create privacy policy: http://www.privacypolicyonline.com/
This is a fast and simple way to generate a privacy policy. You enter the basic information about your web site, provide the URL, and a policy is generated which you can put on your web site. The site is user-friendly and can quickly generate a policy specific to your web site.

Beyond the mere obligation, these legal notices are there to reassure users of our website / application. It is therefore important to respect the relevant policies and legislation.

5.2 Declaration to a data protection authorities

Data protection authorities are authorities tasked with the protection of data and privacy of Internet users.

Below is a list of some data protection authorities:
- ✓ **United States**: Federal Trade Commission
- ✓ **United Kingdom**: the Information Commissioner's Office
- ✓ **Germany**: the Federal Commissioner for Data Protection and Freedom of Information

- ✓ **France**: the Commission nationale de l'informatique et des libertés

From the moment our website / application processes personal data, it is necessary to declare to the data protection authorities of our country. They will give us a declaration number to be included in the legal notice page.

Are exempted from declaration:
- Personal blogs or website/applications.
- Showcase website/applications.
- Association's websites/applications.

5.3 Personal information gathering

Any person being subject to a collection of information must be clearly **informed**, and his choice must be **voluntary**. The addresses intended for the commercial prospecting cannot be collected in a public space (on a forum, a directory, a discussion...).

The Data Protection Act gives rights to individuals in respect of the personal data that organizations hold about them. This is the sixth data protection principle, and the rights of individuals that it refers to are:
- **The right of access** to a copy of the information comprised in their personal data;
- **The right to object** to processing that is likely to cause or is causing damage or distress;
- **The right to prevent** processing for direct marketing;
- **The right to object** to decisions being taken by automated means;
- **The right** in certain circumstances to have inaccurate personal data **rectified, blocked, erased** or **destroyed**;
- **The right to claim compensation** for damages caused by a breach of the Act.

In addition, during the prospection, each newsletter sent to registrants must offer them the possibility to unsubscribe at any time.

5.4 Business structure

Of all the decisions we make when starting a business, probably the most important one relating to taxes is the type of legal structure we select for our company.

Not only will this decision have an impact on how much we pay in taxes, but it will affect the amount of paperwork our business is required to do, the personal liability we face and your ability to raise money.

Table Comparing the Different Forms of Business

Type of Business	Sole Proprietorship	Partnerships		Corporations		Limited Liability Company
		General	Limited	C Corp	S Corp	
Definition	A business owned and operated by one person for profit.	Two or more people who jointly own or operate a business for profit.	One or more partners have limited liability and no rights of management.	An organization formed under state or federal law. An artificial entity separate from its owners.	An organization structured like a corporation but taxed like a partnership.	A business entity created by statute. The owners are called members. It is taxed like a partnership or an s corp. It has limited liability like corporations.
Ease of Formation	Easiest form of business to set up. If necessary, acquire licenses and permits, register fictitious name, and obtain taxpayer identification.	Easy to set up and operate. A written partnership agreement is highly recommended. Must acquire an Employer ID number. If necessary, register fictitious name.	File a Certificate of Limited Partnership with the Secretary of State. Name must show that business is a limited partnership. Must have written agreement, and must	File articles of incorporation and other required reports with the Secretary of State. Prepare bylaws and follow corporate formalities.	Must meet all criteria to file as an S corporation. Must file timely election with the IRS (within 21/2 months of first taxable year).	File articles of organization with the Secretary of State. Adopt operating agreement, and file necessary reports with Secretary of State. The name must show it is

			keep certain records.			limited liability company.
Period of Existence	Terminates at will or on the death of the owner.	Terminates by agreement, or by death or withdrawal of partner, unless there is a partnership agreement to the contrary.		Continues until formal dissolution. Most stable form of business. Not affected by death or disaffiliation of shareholder.		May terminate by agreement, or withdrawal of a member, depending upon operating agreement.
Taxes	Profits are taxed once. Profit and loss are reported on the owner's individual state and federal income tax returns.	Profits are taxed once. Each partner reports his or her share of the profit and loss on his or her individual state and federal income tax returns. Partnership files an information return.		Profits are subject to double taxation, once at the corporate level, and again at the shareholder level.	Profits are taxed once. Each shareholder reports his or her share of profit and loss on individual income tax returns. S corp does not pay tax, with some exceptions.	If the LLC is structured properly, each member reports his or her share of the profit and loss on his or her individual income tax returns. It is taxed like a partnership or an S corp. If the LLC is not structured properly, it is taxed like a C corporation.
Liability	The owner's personal assets are at risk.	Each partner's personal assets are at risk.	General partners' personal assets are at risk. A limited partner is liable only to	Limited to corporate assets, except: 1. Personally guaranteed business debts; 2. Personal negligence or fault; or 3. Corporate form is found		Similar to rules for corporations.

			the extent of his or her investment.	to be a sham.	
Dissolution	Easiest form of business to dissolve. Pay debts, taxes, and claims against business.	Pay debts, taxes, and claims against business. Settle partnership accounts.	Pay debts, taxes, and claims against business. Settle partnership accounts. File cancellation of certificate with the Secretary of State.	Obtain shareholder approval to dissolve. File statement of intent to dissolve with the Secretary of State. Pay debts, taxes, and claims against business. Distribute corporate assets to shareholders.	Pay debts, taxes, and claims against business. Distribute remaining assets to members. File articles of dissolution with the Secretary of State.
				Gain on distribution of assets is subject to double taxation.	Gain on distribution of assets is taxed once, with some exceptions.	

6. The publication of website/application

6.1 Website hosting

In order to publish a website online, we need a Web host. The Web host stores all the pages of our website and makes them available to computers connected to the Internet. It is strongly advisable to use a hosting service offering secured servers permanently connected to Internet at very high speed (hundreds of Mb/s).

6.1.1 Web Hosting Types

There are various types of web hosting services available to host your website. Before signing up for web hosting services, it is important to understand what kind of service your website needs, the kind of server you or your business needs, your budget, and what type of services the web host offers.

- **Free Hosting**: free web hosting is best suited for small sites with low traffic. It is not recommended for high traffic or for real business. Technical support is often limited, and technical options are few.
- **Shared Hosting**: with shared hosting, our website is hosted on a powerful server along with many other web sites. Shared solutions often offer multiple software solutions like e-mail, database, and different editing options. Technical support tends to be good.
- **Dedicated Hosting**: we have the entire web server to ourselves. This allows for faster performance, as we have all the server's resources entirely, without sharing with other website owners. However, this also means that we will be responsible for the cost of server operation entirely. This is a good choice for websites that requires a lot of system resources, or need a higher level of security.
- **Collocated Hosting**: in this type of hosting, we will purchase our own server and have it housed at a web host's facilities. We will be responsible for the server itself. An advantage of this type of hosting service is we

have full control of the web server and we can install any scripts or applications we need.

6.1.2 Selection criteria

Once you've decided on the type of hosting plan, consider these issues in choosing a specific provider:

- **Cost:** While it's important to look for a hosting provider that offers reasonable rates, avoid free hosting programs entirely, as they may be unreliable and their low costs are often subsidized by required on-site advertisements.
- **Customer reviews:** Customer reviews can be an excellent resource in evaluating web hosts because any fly-by-night host can put up a professional-looking sales page and make bold promises. Search for multiple reviews from current or past customers because a single positive review could have originated from the company's own marketing department.
- **Customer support.** Whether you're a beginning webmaster or a more experienced digital business owner, you'll want a dependable customer support team behind your web hosting plan. Things can and will go wrong on your website's backend, but getting support when you need it can go a long way toward minimizing any potential damage to your business. Look for companies that provide 24/7 phone support, email access and online chat. Before committing to a plan, test out each of these features to get a feel for how well your needs will be met.
- **Storage and bandwidth allowances.** As more hosting plans begin offering unlimited disk space and bandwidth, this may not be a concern for your business. But it's still important to be aware of any limitations to ensure that your plan has enough space for your website to operate effectively.
- **Script support.** One final consideration is the hosting company's built-in support for popular web scripts. Say, for example, you want to run WordPress on your website. Some hosts offer built-in script packages that make the installation of this popular blogging platform a breeze. Other

hosts limit the number of MySQL databases that can be created, which you'll need to run WordPress and other programs.

6.1.3   Some web hosting providers

Following a list of some good web hosting companies (free and paid):

- **Paid hosting providers**: iPage, BlueHost, JustHost, WebHostingHub, HostMonster, HostGator, Arvixe, FatCow, SiteGround, GoDaddy, InMotion, Dreamhost.
- **Free hosting providers**: Wix, Weebly, Yola, 000webhost, EDUBlogs, Freehostia, Webs, 5GBfree, Jimdo, FreeHosting, SnapPages, 110MB, AwardSpace, 1FreeHosting, Zymic, FreeHostingEU.

6.2   Publication of the mobile application:

6.2.1   Publishing on App Store

Once developed, the application must submit application for approval. It is then added to the App Store, with the payment of a license ($99 USD per year for an individual, $299 USD per year for a company).

Learn more: http://www.apple.com/itunes/sellcontent/

6.2.2   Publishing on Google Play

To distribute an application through Google Play, a developer account must be created. This only needs to be performed once, and does involve a one time fee of $25 USD.

Learn more: https://play.google.com/apps/publish/signup/

6.2.3   Publishing on Windows Phone Store

To publish and distribute an application via Windows Phone Store, a developer account must be created, and requires only a one-time registration payment ($19 for individual accounts and $99 for company accounts).

Learn more: https://dev.windowsphone.com/en-us/publish

7. Increase website/application traffic

7.1 Introduction

If we aren't attracting visitors, our website is bound to get lost in the vastness of the Internet and perhaps, never found. Every site needs traffic, and even if our site is made very well, if we are not attracting visitors, we won't be generating sales or achieving our end goal with our startup.

Below are some tips we can follow to increase traffic to our website (also valid to promote mobile applications):

7.2 Natural SEO (Search Engine Optimization)

Search engine optimization (SEO) is the practice of manipulating aspects of a Website to improve its **ranking** in search engines. Various approaches are taken to achieve that goal, such as **submitting** the Website to directory services, and addressing Web site architecture and content:
- **Submission** is how a Webmaster submits a website directly to a search engine.
- **Ranking** is the position at which a particular website appears in the results of a search engine query.

Methods to achieve high rankings in the organic results can be divided into two categories and dedicated SEO experts are well versed in these two categories. The first is on page optimization. It includes the care of things like keyword density, title tag optimization, keywords in the content, keywords in hyperlinks, the quality of original content, keywords in bold labels and headings, the keywords in the URL, meta tags, site maps, link structure, etc. The second is indexability of the page optimization. It includes the care of such factors as the amount of incoming links, quality and relevance of websites that link to yours, keywords in anchor text, etc.

Pros
- **It's free**: Search engines don't charge to have our website/application come up in results. However, it takes a lot of time and effort to develop the most relevant web presence.
- SEO rankings have greater **credibility**. People trust organic results a lot more than paid advertising. They are much more likely to click on organic listings than on a paid ad.
- SEO work done benefits our rankings in every search engine, from Google and Bing to small ones we've never heard of, and even in search engines that have not yet been created.

Cons
- **Lack of Control**: there are a lot of factors and elements that are out of our control when dealing with organic results.
- **Unknown Factors**: Google is fairly secretive about what they use a formula for "relevant" sites. While we do know some general "best practices" Google likes to see, it's not 100% clear what will drive our page to the top.
- **Long-Term Investment**: SEO takes longer to see results – benefits of SEO work is measured in months, and it can take several months before we begin to see measurable results.
- The **competition is strong** in some areas and the 1st page is only 10 positions.

Submit the website
It is important to submit our website's pages to all of the major search engines (Google, Yahoo, Bing) because even though the other engines have less traffic than Google, they still have millions of users. When we submit a

URL or domain name to the search engines, it could take anywhere from two to four weeks to get indexed.

- Google: https://www.google.com/webmasters/tools/submit-url
- Bing: http://www.bing.com/toolbox/submit-site-url
- Yahoo: http://search.yahoo.com/info/submit.html
- DMOZ: http://www.dmoz.org
- Voilà: http://referencement.ke.voila.fr/

SEO optimization
Following some tips to increase our search engine ranking:
- An original and attractive content,
- A well chosen title,
- An appropriate URL,
- A readable text by search engines,
- Meta tags to describe the content of the page,
- Thoughtful links,
- ALT attributes to describe the content of images,
- Create a sitemap.

Useful tools
- Google Webmaster Tools: https://www.google.com/webmasters/tools/
- Google Trends: http://www.google.fr/trends/
- ÜberSuggest - Get keyword ideas: http://ubersuggest.org/
- To analyze a website and who's linking to it: http://www.opensiteexplorer.org/
- Check PageRank and other SEO statistics: http://checkpagerank.net/

7.3 Pay Per Click (PPC)

PPC (pay-per-click) marketing is a form of online advertising in which advertisers accrue costs when users click their ads. Advertisers bid on keywords and audience types, which a search engine matches to user search queries and predefined lists, and then displays ads.

PPC is all about relevance. Users are searching for specific products, services, and information at any given time. Advertisers have the ability to show a targeted ad at the exact moment this search is occurring.

Pros
- **Instant traffic to our website:** pay-per-click gives us the ability to have ads on the top of search results almost immediately after setting up a PPC campaign.
- **Full control:** we are in complete control of our ad copy, the keywords that will trigger our ad and the destination URL that the visitor is sent to after they click on our ad.
- **No worrying about algorithm updates:** PPC ads are not impacted like the organic (unpaid) search results are when search engines perform an algorithm update.
- **Ability to set our own budget**: With PPC, we can define exactly how much money we want to spend. In Adwords, for instance, we can set a daily budget. Once our budget has been reached, our ads will no longer display for the rest of the day.
- **Target specific regions**: with PPC platforms, we can display our ads to a specific state or city.

Cons
- **Can be very expensive:** pay-per-click can be very expensive if the campaign is not correctly set up, resulting in a depleted budget with little to nothing to show from it.
- **Must optimize constantly:** paid search marketing is not a "set it and forget it" advertising option, as PPC campaigns require constant optimization and fine tuning in order to keep the ads performing and producing a ROI.
- **Bidding wars:** when two or more PPC advertisers compete for a top ad position, it can turn into a costly "bidding war" where no one wins.

- **Click fraud**: there's a very real possibility of click fraud. This occurs when PPC advertisers barrage their competitors' ads with fake clicks from different IP addresses, racking up expensive bills from ghost traffic.

Learn more: http://adwords.google.fr

7.4 Get social

It's not enough to produce great content and hope that people find it – we have to be proactive. One of the best ways to increase traffic to our application is to use social media channels to promote our content.

The use of social networks (such as Facebook, Twitter, Google+, LinkedIn, YouTube…) proves to be a powerful web-marketing lever due to its viral effect.

Most are free and the fact to network with other users (professional contacts, friends, colleagues…) is a great way to make known our application and increase its traffic.

Pros
- This is a quick technique to implement.
- Cost is more likely to be less than search engine traffic both in time and money.

Cons
- The traffic is quite limited.
- All social networks do not have a good image.

Tips
- **Facebook**: allows us to create a page for our startup to quickly share new articles with a large number of people, as well as share other related articles.

- **Twitter**: allows us to create an account for our business and post the headline and link to each new article we publish. Many blogging software packages allow us to do this automatically.
- **Tumblr:** is a blogging service that allows us to easily link to content around the web. We can use Tumblr to post links to our articles as well as related content.
- **Google+**: is Google's social network service, and has a very large potential audience, since all Google users have access to it.
- **Pinterest**: is an image-focused social sharing site.
- **Instagram**: allows us to create an account for our startup and take some pictures related to our niche.
- **Reddit** and **Digg**: both have large communities of active users. Posting our article can result in a lot of good traffic and sharing, as long as we are posting in the correct place and following submission rules.

7.5 E-mailing

Emailing or **E-mailing** is a method of direct marketing, which uses electronic mail as a means of commercial communication to send messages to an audience in order to present a business, product or service

Pros
- Inexpensive: The cost is very low compared to sending a paper mailing by post.
- Fast: Just a few seconds to send a message while it takes several days for a paper mailing.
- Proactive: It is you who take the initiative to send an email. You don't wait for a search or a click on an ad.
- Targeted: It is possible to send a targeted message to all or part of the data base and targeting on specific criteria.

Cons
- Spam problem.

- Open rate (the number of list subscribers who opened the e-mail message) varies according to the business areas.
- The increasing disinterest of users.
- Cost of a well-qualified database.
- Limited size of email attachments.

7.6 The Video Marketing

Videos are becoming more and more important on the Internet as more users gain access to faster Internet connections. It is because of this that startups need to start thinking about video SEO and the strategy behind marketing video content on the Internet. Videos are especially important in helping drive traffic to our website/application. Search engines recognize that videos usually offer high quality content, and take time and effort to produce.

Here are just a few statistics regarding the efficacy of video marketing:
- Videos increase people's understanding of your product or service by 74%.
- More than 6 billion hours of video are watched each month on YouTube.
- More than 1 billion unique users visit YouTube each month.
- Website visitors are 64% more likely to buy a product on an online retail site after watching a video.

Pros
- Extremely easy to manage the videos.
- Massive audience.
- Bigger chance to rank in search engines.
- Cost-free.

Cons

- Hard to target the right audience.
- Issues with copyright and piracy.
- Regional restrictions.
- Advertisement (sometimes form competitors).

7.7 Create a blog for website/mobile application

Adding a blog to our site can drastically increase the amount of highly targeted traffic our site gets.

A startup's blog is a form of content marketing. The idea is pretty simple. We identify what questions people in our target audience are wondering about or asking each other about. Then we create blog posts (articles) that explain the answers to those questions.

People will start finding those blog posts in the search results when they are searching around looking for the answers to those questions. When they click on that listing in the search results, they are taken to our blog post on our website. Once they are there, we can get them to notice that we sell a product or service that is directly relevant to what they are looking for.

7.8 Promote dialogue

As we know, there are three ways to access a website: directly enter the address (URL) in a browser, use a search engine or surf from link to link. To increase traffic to our website, we need to facilitate better either (or all) of these approaches. Concretely, we must communicate as widely as possible the address of our site, optimize our placement in search engines and a maximum spread of links on the web.

The Internet is a space for dialogue. Forum, websites, blogs ... are many places where it is possible to communicate the address of our website. The link exchange is a technique commonly used by webmasters. Targeting sites with a hearing in accordance with our target, we will ensure qualified traffic.

We should start participating actively in forums and blogs on our theme, answer questions, initiate discussions, comment on posts, offer our help, indicating the address of our website ...

7.9 Viral Marketing

Viral marketing is an online marketing technique which involves creating an infectious excitement about our product so that people pass on information about it through emails, social networking sites, blogs and any other form of online network.

The theory behind the value of Internet viral marketing is that the message can be received by exponential numbers of potential customers. For example, if I forward your message to 10 friends and each of those 10 friends forwards the message to 10 other friends, the message could spread very rapidly.

YouTube is probably the best example of Internet viral marketing. If a video is very funny, unusual or provokes certain emotions, it's likely that the video will become popular quickly. Links to the video will quickly multiply as viewers share the video with others. Many may even decide to embed the video (if permitted) in various places on the Internet, drawing even more attention.

7.10 Conclusion

These techniques well known by web marketers are all complementary and need to be foreseen for a global web marketing strategy. They can increase traffic to our website/application: massive traffic or more qualified. To measure the returns and the relevance of these techniques, we should implement a web analytics tool.

8. Web analytics

8.1 Definition

Web analytics is the process of analyzing the behavior of visitors to a Web site. It allows to quantify the traffic of a website based on indicators like the number of unique visitors, page views, traffic sources, etc. It combines the measurement, collection, analysis and reporting of Internet data for the purposes of understanding and optimizing Web usage.

8.2 Web Analytics: Metrics & Key Performance Indicators

Here's a list of the most important indicators and metrics we should use to measure our website traffic:

Building Block: foundational metrics
- **Page**: a page is an analyst definable unit of content.
- **Page Views**: the number of times a page was viewed
- **Visits/Sessions**: A visit is an interaction by an individual, with a website consisting of one or more requests for a page.
- **Unique Visitors**: The number of inferred individual people, within a designated reporting timeframe, with activity consisting of one or more visits to a site.

- o **New Visitor**: The number of Unique Visitors with activity including a first-ever Visit to a site during a reporting period
- o **Repeat Visitor**: The number of Unique Visitors with activity consisting of two or more Visits to a site during a reporting period.
- o **Return Visitor**: The number of Unique Visitors with activity consisting of a Visit to a site during a reporting period and where the Unique Visitor also Visited the site prior to the reporting period.

Visit Characterization: metrics to understand visits (single or aggregate)
- **Entry Page**: The first page of a visit.
- **Landing Page**: A page intended to identify the beginning of the user experience.
- **Exit Page**: The last page on a site accessed during a visit, signifying the end of a visit/session.
- **Visit Duration**: The length of time in a session.
- **Referrer**: The referrer is the page URL that originally generated the request for the current page view or object.
- **Click-through**: Number of times a link was clicked by a visitor.
- **Click-through Rate**: The number of click-throughs for a specific link divided by the number of times that link was viewed.
- **Page Views per Visit**: The number of page views in a reporting period divided by number of visits in the same reporting period.

Content Characterization: metrics aimed at understanding content or its use
- **Page Exit Ratio**: Number of exits from a page divided by total number of page views of that page
- **Single Page Visits**: Visits that consist of one page regardless of the number of times the page was viewed.
- **Single Page View Visits** (Bounces): Visits that consist of one page-view .
- **Bounce Rate**: Single page view visits divided by entry pages.

Conversion: metrics aimed at linking visits and content
- **Event**: Any logged or recorded action that has a specific date and time assigned to it by either the browser or server
- **Conversion**: A visitor completing a target action

8.3 Web Analytics tools

There are plenty of web analytics tools available on the market, all with different features and benefits.

Here is a quick review of most popular of them to help you decide which one will work best for you.

8.3.1 Google Analytics

By far the most popular web analytics tool is Google Analytics. Google Analytics is geared toward Internet marketers and small business owners who want to learn more about their website. Google Analytics helps marketers and website owners understand traffic patterns, traffic sources, conversions, bounce rates, paid search statistics, and more. The data available is robust and intuitive enough for anyone to learn. While it is intuitive, there is a bit of a learning curve, and you may need to take a few tutorials in order to really get the full benefits of Google Analytics.

Pros
- The Cost: Google Analytics is free
- Advanced features
- Ecommerce tracking
- Constantly evolving tool

- Simple integration
- Contains no advertising

Cons
- No real support.
- Shares data with Google.
- Some ad filtering programs have the capability to block the Google Analytics tracking code. This means you may not receive data on some of your visitors.

Cost: Free
Link: http://www.google.com/analytics/

8.3.2 Piwik

Piwik is a free, open-source analytics application developed using PHP and MySQL. It has a "plugins" system that allows for utmost extensibility and customization.

Install only the plugins you need or go overboard and install them all – the choice is up to you.

The plugins system, as you can imagine, also opens up possibilities for you to create your own custom extensions. The download is only 1.9MB.

Pros
- It has a plugin mechanism so it's customizable.
- It stores data on your server so you get control of the data and it is not shared with any third party.
- It has a customizable user interface.
- Ranks top keywords and provides real time traffic reports.
- Lets you block traffics, URLs and IP addresses.
- Data can be exported in many file formats, such as PHP, Excel and XML.
- Deletes old data automatically.
- Allows segmentation and makes it possible to request any subset for Piwik reports.

- Dashboard can be customized according to your needs.
- Can track many websites.

Cons
- No real support (only community forums).
- Lack of advanced features.
- Greedy in resources (disk space, database)

Cost: Free
Link: http://piwik.org/

8.3.3 Clicky

Clicky is considered to be one of the most robust web analytics tool today and it provides real time traffic information of your website. The main dashboard includes a variety of website stats that can be customized based on date. It offers a link report that shows all external websites sending traffic to you. It offers an actions metric that measures all visitor actions like video views and downloads by the user. It offers search data which provides a list of incoming search keywords that brought the users to your website and, with its Sheer SEO tool, Clicky also shows the ranking for those keywords.

Pros
- Its analytics feature is nearly as good as Google Analytics.
- It provides real-time data so you don't have to wait the following day to find out what's going on with your website today.
- Unlike other free tracking tools it is very easy to install. Infact, wordpress users can install it with a simple plugin.
- Clicky automatically feeds your website with keywords people are using to access it; plus, it shows your ranking as well.
- It offers an interesting feature called Twitter Search Tracking, with which you can monitor twitter tags, keywords and retweets.

- It also has an iPhone app called ClickyTouch which gives allows you to stay updated right from your mobile device.
- A robust API for advanced users.
- Heat Maps included.
- Split-testing and A/B Testing features are also present

Cons
- Its interface is not user-friendly. First-time users may find it overwhelming.
- It will require you to pay a fee if you install it on multiple sites or if your site gets more than 3000 page views a day.
- Many key features such as goal tracking and email reports are only available in premium accounts.

Costs: Its pricing depends on the page views. You can find more specific pricing info here (http://clicky.com/help/pricing). It also offers a 21-day free trial for all accounts.

Link: http://clicky.com/

8.3.4 Woopra

Woopra is also a real-time website analysis tool that targets customer engagement. It offers top-notch analytics that allows you to seamlessly monitor more than one website simultaneously.

Pros
- On its online app, When you click on the number of visitors on your website, it shows exactly what those visitors are individually doing on your site.
- It has a really good UI and a very well thought dashboard, for advanced webmasters.
- It lets you view activities on your site in real-time.

- It lets you track blog posts, comments, and searches through its WP plugin.
- It also features live chat, which allows you to talk to your customers when they're on your site.
- Goes one step ahead and brings you customer insights from website visitors ie It tells you how the website is being used, instead of who is using the website.

Cons
- The dashboards have so much of data (which is a good thing) but it can be confusing for beginners.
- Managing multiple sites using sub-folders is slightly difficult for new users.

Costs: $0 to $199.95/month, depending on how large your website is. Free for up to 30,000 actions per month.

Link: http://www.woopra.com/

8.3.5 AWStats

AWStats is considered to be one of the most amazing web analysis tools on the Web that will analyze log files coming from services such as HTTP, FTP servers and streaming media. Their main interface consists of a single page that is divided into different sections, each providing a summary of statistical data. These include daily visits, list of referrers, search terms etc. These stats are automatically updated on a daily basis. It gives you the option of viewing a month-by-month traffic report, or you could also view the annual statistics.

AWStats defines a visitor on the basis of the user agent and IP address. If someone visits your website with a user agent, for example Google Chrome, and has an IP address, it will be counted as a unique visitor. On the other hand, if the user agent is a robot, such as GoogleBot, it will not be counted as a visitor.

Pros
- It will tell you the number of hits you have on your website, including the number of unique visitors as well as the time they spent on your website.
- It will show you how much bandwidth different crawlers and robots are using.
- It will tell you which countries, your traffic originated from.
- It has a feature called Server Side, which can effectively process Raw Log files.
- It can support various file types.
- It allows you to view web compression stats.
- It displays common HTTP errors.
- It is open-source.

Cons
- It does not provide an in-depth analysis of data so it is recommended that you use this alongside other tools.
- Although Awstats identifies most common bots and avoids the mistake of counting it as a visitor, there are some bots it is still not familiar with, thus, incorrectly counting them as visitors and causing discrepancies in the visitor count.
- It does not measure user activity. There is no way to know what the user does once they are on your site.
- A visitor that accesses the same website on different IP addresses, at the same time, will be counted as more than one visitor.
- It does not have a cookie system in place to determine the visitor count when two users visit the website from the same IP address; instead, it uses a time frame of 60 minutes to measure a visit. If a user visits the website for 20 minutes and visits again after 40 minutes, it will still be counted as one visit. But instead, if they visit 45 minutes later, it will be counted as two visits.
- It does not give an option to narrow down statistics to a more specific time frame, for example, last 7 days.
- The UI reminds us of the Late 90s.

Costs: $0 (Some hosting providers offer this as a freebie).

Link: http://www.awstats.org/

8.3.6 AT Internet

AT Internet is an advanced analytics tool designed to make it easy for Webmasters to analyze and measure their website's data.

It offers a comprehensive suite including Web, social and mobile analytics in real time, serving more than 3,500 customers worldwide: Total, Maroc Telecom, Accor, Euro sport, etc.

Pros
- Analysis of navigation, traffic, sources, behavior, goals, technology, geo-location.
- Proprietary technology called ClickZone (combinations of heatmaps and overlay) which helps improve user experience.
- Multivariate testing feature available.
- Measure user interaction with Rich media.
- Performance and uptime monitoring included.
- It comes with advanced analytics reporting features including an intuitive interface that allows you to cross-analyze multiple categories and export in various formats.
- An option to create Custom metrics.
- Advanced analytics reporting features.
- Complete view of e-marketing campaigns and their profitability.
- Offers behavioral analysis to better target the audience.
- Tracks email campaigns.

Cons
- Pricing not available on website.

Link: http://www.atinternet.com/

9. Funding

Taking a business from idea to reality involves a good deal of attrition, ingenuity, and compromise. But no matter how much these three factors align in your favor, chances are you won't get far unless you have some sort of funding.

Several solutions are available:

9.1 Fund your startup yourself

These days, the costs to start a business are at an all-time low, and over 90 percent of startups are self funded (also called bootstrapping). It may take a bit longer to save some money before you start and grow organically, but the advantage is that you don't have to give up any equity or control. Your business is yours alone.

9.2 Pitch your needs to friends and family

As a general rule, professional investors will expect that you have already have commitments from this source to show your credibility. If your friends and family don't believe in you, don't expect outsiders to jump in. This is the primary source of non-personal funds for very early-stage startups.

9.3 Request a small-business grant

These are government funds allocated to support new technologies and important causes, such as education, medicine and social needs. A good place to start looking is Grants.gov, which is a searchable directory of more than 1,000 federal grant programs. The process is long, but it doesn't cost you any equity.

9.4 Seek a bank loan or credit-card line of credit

In general, this won't happen for a new startup unless you have a good credit history or existing assets that you are willing to put at risk for collateral. In the U.S., you may find that the Small Business Administration (SBA) can get you infusions of cash without normal backup requirements.

9.5 Start a crowdfunding campaign online

This newest source of funding, where anyone can participate per the jobs act, is exemplified by online sites such as Kickstarter. Here people make online pledges to your startup during a campaign, to pre-buy the product for later delivery, give donations or qualify for a reward, such as a T-shirt.

9.6 Solicit investors

These are professional investors, such as Accel Partners, who invest institutional money in qualified startups, usually with a proven business model, ready to scale. They typically look for big opportunities, needing a couple of million dollars or more, with a proven team. Look for a warm introduction to make this work.

9.7 Join a startup incubator or accelerator

These organizations are very popular these days, and are often associated with major universities, community development organizations, or even large companies. Most provide free resources to startups, including office facilities and consulting, but many provide seed funding as well.

9.8 Enter a competition

Start-ups are using competitions as a way to scoop up much-needed funds in the crucial formative stage.

Competitions don't just provide funds of course – they can offer even more valuable intangibles, such as mentoring, networking or even just a first-hand lesson on how you should pitch your business to potential investors or clients.

Here's a list of the most popular competitions from around the world:
- The Million Pound Startup
- Startmate
- Global StartCamp
- MassChallenge
- Women 2.0
- Enterprize Business Plan Competition

10. Business models (monetization)

Once you have a website (or mobile app) that is regularly updated and gets a steady amount of traffic, you should start thinking about monetizing.

Monetizing your website essentially means to add things to it or make certain changes that will help your website make money or become profitable. There are hundreds of ways to monetize your website, and some of them are simple while others are more complex and costly.

As with most strategies regarding money, diversification is key. Try a combination of these methods to maximize earning potential (some examples of monetization strategies: http://rcs.seerinteractive.com/money/)

Ready to start monetizing your content? Let's go...

10.1 Paid app

This is the classic and proven monetization method for mobile applications, well known both by users and publishers. Some apps priced below one dollar have had a staggering success.

- The model is very straightforward, the revenue is proportional to the downloads.
- 70% for the developer / 30% for the platform
- Pricing can be different from one OS to the other
- Some users may be reluctant to buy apps, mainly on Android
- With paid apps, you are less likely to reach a lot of users

10.2 Pay Per Click Advertising Networks

One of the most popular methods of monetizing a site, blog or mobile app is to sell advertising space, usually banner ads. You could manage this manually, but it is much more efficient to either use a network or a plugin/resource that will automate much of the process.

Google AdSense is the most popular option under this category, but there are also others. Basically you need to sign up with the network and paste some code snippets on your website. The network will then serve contextual ads (either text or images) relevant to your website, and you will earn a certain amount of money for every click.

List of popular PPC advertising networks:
- **Google Adsense**: www.google.com/adsense
- **Yahoo Publisher Network**: contextualads.yahoo.net
- **BuySellAds**: buysellads.com
- **BidVertiser**: bidvertiser.com
- **Chitika**: chitika.com
- **Clicksor**: clicksor.com

10.3 Affiliate Marketing

Affiliate marketing is a very popular way to make money through your application. In short, you sell (or recommend) someone else's product(s) on your website/mobile app. When your visitor clicks on your affiliate link and buys the product – you'll receive commission.

The commission is usually 30% – 70% of the product or service price. So if you promote an e-book that costs $100, you'll get $50 for referring the buyer (just an example).

Where can we find products to promote?
- **Commission** junction: reliable, payments on time.
- **ShareASale**: mostly clothes and accessories.
- **Clickbank**: high payouts, but lack of good products to promote.
- **Link Share**

10.4 Set up an online store

You don't always have to create a website about something. You can just create a "tool" for your business – an online store.

If you have enough dedication to make it work, try it out. Be aware of the competition, though. There are thousands of e-commerce website on the Internet, but only few of them make a lot of money. Plan out your strategy, keep your design up-do-date and use the latest marketing techniques.

10.5 Services/Consulting/Coaching

Another great way to make money with an app is an indirect one. Use your website/mobile app to build reputation. Build a brand and build an audience. Then, you make your money by directing that attention into offline services, consulting and/or coaching. This can be quite lucrative. The drawback is that you are, again, trading time for money. So, it is only scalable up to a point.

10.6 Data Monetization

Websites and mobile apps contain valuable user data that can be monetized through various methods. Data generated by websites about their users can range from being demographics to in-market data (i.e. in-market for a car).

This data can be sold through behavioral data exchanges and used by advertisers to target their online media campaigns. Websites can also generate revenue from their newsletter and on-site registrations programs by helping to bring in offline data associated with users during this process.

10.7 Freemium

Popular with many games and some service-oriented applications, the "freemium" model is a huge and growing trend in online income right now. You provide a lot of quality content for free to your audience, and you provide a premium-level program to those willing to pay for it. You charge a monthly membership and that provides continuity and a steady income stream.

10.8 Sell your application to someone else

Website/mobile application selling is becoming a very lucrative business model. If you are into short-term projects and more into "quick buck" you can implement it as well.

The site value is usually based on the income. If your website is making $500 per/month through selling ad space, you can sell the site for $5,000 – $10,000 (12x – 22x monthly income).

Where can we sell an app?
- **Flippa**: The most popular website market.
- **Digitalpoint**: Free forum.
- **FEinternational**: Mostly for high-end websites.

10.9 Donation / Becoming a sponsor

Setting up donation buttons or simply asking additional funds from your readers is another way to monetize your website. It's easy to set up, but you have to be aware that it's not so easy to make money with it. Unless you find a sponsor(s) who pays a lot! However, before you throw up your donation buttons and widgets, make sure that your visitors will see why you need those donations (hosting expenses, new product creation, researching costs etc…).